Blue Christmas
A Guided Retreat to Ease Your Heartache and Bring Peace of Mind

"Twinkle" Marie Manning

Matrika Press

Blue Christmas
A Guided Retreat
to Ease Your Heartache and Bring Peace of Mind

Copyright © "Twinkle" Marie Manning
November 2020, December 2025

All Rights Reserved
including the right of reproduction,
copying, or storage in any form
or means, including electronic,
In Whole or Part,
without prior written
permission of the author.

ISBN: 978-1-946088-27-7

1. Journal 2. Self Care 3. Self-Exploration
4. Spirituality 5. Philosophy 6. Christmas. 7. Keepsake
8. Title

Matrika Press
www.MatrikaPress.com

www.TwinklesPlace.org
#LivingLifeAsAPrayer
#PulpitOfPeace

The contents of this book are for informational, educational and spiritual exploration purposes only. Always seek the advice of your physician or other qualified mental health providers with any questions you may have regarding a medical condition, mental health concerns, and for professional psychological, psychiatric or medical advice, diagnosis, or treatment.

If you are feeling suicidal, thinking about hurting yourself, or are concerned that someone you know may be in danger of hurting themselves, call the **National Suicide Prevention Lifeline at 1-800-273-8255.** It is available 24 hours a day, 7 days a week and is staffed by certified crisis response professionals.

Please seek help if you need it.
Your life has value.
You are needed and wanted on Earth.
You are a blessing to the world,
even if and when you do not feel like you are.

Love,
Twinkle

Introduction

Blue Christmas, A Guided Retreat to Ease Your Heartache and Bring Peace of Mind is designed to be used as a self-led retreat to guide you in quiet reflective moments during the holiday season. It is where you can contemplate and document your inner-most thoughts, feelings and beliefs.

Holidays can be emotional and challenging times laden with sadness, worry and fear. Stress and heartache, especially grief, are often amplified. The holidays, while filled with light, can create palpable darkness. This *Blue Christmas* book is where you can hold your grief sacred throughout the holiday season.

How to Use the Blue Christmas Blessing Book:
There are prompts to serve as guides for you to contemplate. You can spin off of these prompts or take your entries in an entirely different direction. Select a word or phrase that is meaningful to you. Place the word or phrase at the top of selected page (and in the corresponding place in the Table of Contents). Use the content space provided on the page to describe its significance. The space is kept intentionally small so as to encourage ease of this writing practice.

Blue Christmas is part of the *Matrika Press Blessing Book series*. *Blessing Books* are created by "Twinkle" Marie Manning and are a source of intentional inspiration to be used to record personal messages in times of contemplation. At the heart of Blessing Books is the desire to share sentiments, messages and stories that we can draw upon as sources of comfort and a reminder that we are loved.

Wherever you are on your journey, may this Blessing Book serve you well.

For more resources and rituals to accompany this book, including Blessing Stones and Ornaments, visit: **www.TwinklesPlace.org/blessing-books**
www.RSOTDE.org/reflection-books

This Blessing Book belongs to:

_____

Occasion:

_____

Date:

_____

Blue Christmas
Table of Contents

1. _____
2. _____
3. _____
4. _____
5. _____
6. _____
7. _____
8. _____
9. _____
10. _____
11. _____
12. _____
13. _____

14. _____
15. _____
16. _____
17. _____
18. _____
19. _____
20. _____
21. _____
22. _____
23. _____
24. _____
25. _____
26. _____
27. _____
28. _____
29. _____
30. _____

Reflections
A Holiday Exercise
Thoughts for Contemplation by the Author

About the Publisher
About the Author
Other Works by this Author
Other Books by Matrika Press
Featured Titles
Resources

*"The trauma said,
'Don't write these poems.
Nobody wants to hear you cry about
the grief inside your bones.'"*

— Andrea Gibson

Too often energy is given to holding in the deepest parts of ourselves. We remain silent so as to not burden others. It is important to process grief, sorrow and fear in ways that free up the energy and restore balance to our lives, and to our relationships.
And, to bring peace of mind.

*What are you holding silent
that is crying to be expressed?*

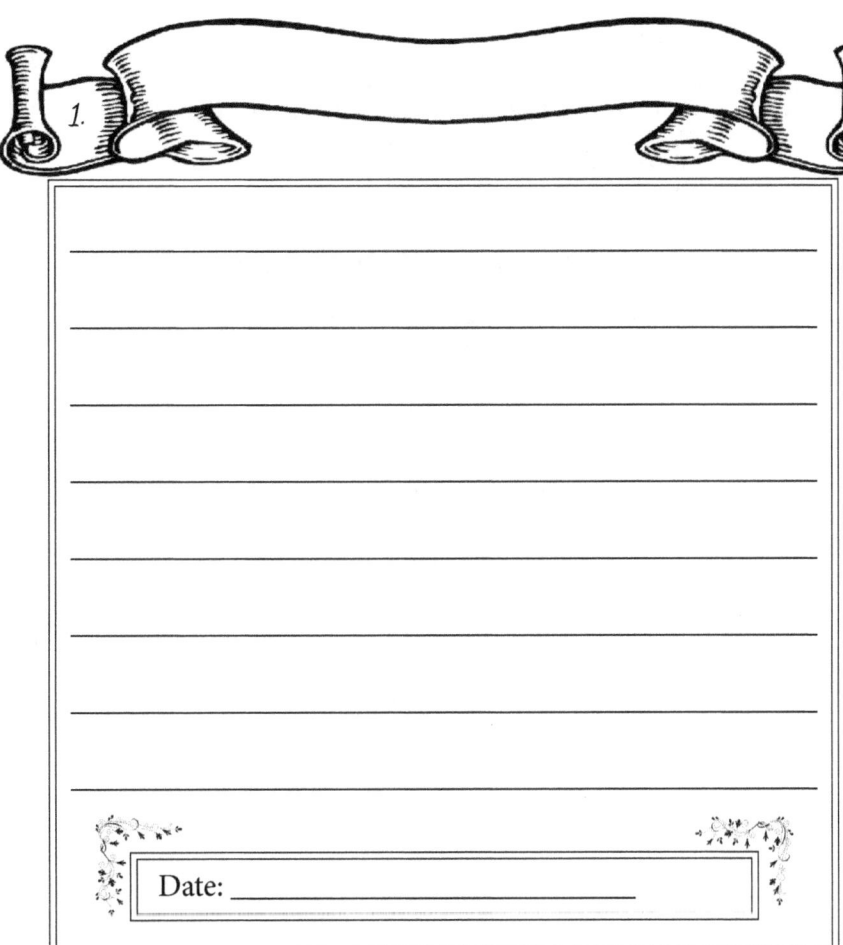

1.

Date: _____

*"Everyone grieves in different ways.
For some, it could take longer or shorter.
I do know it never disappears.
An ember still smolders inside me.
Most days, I don't notice it, but,
out of the blue,
it'll flare to life."*

― Maria V. Snyder

What stage of grief are you at?

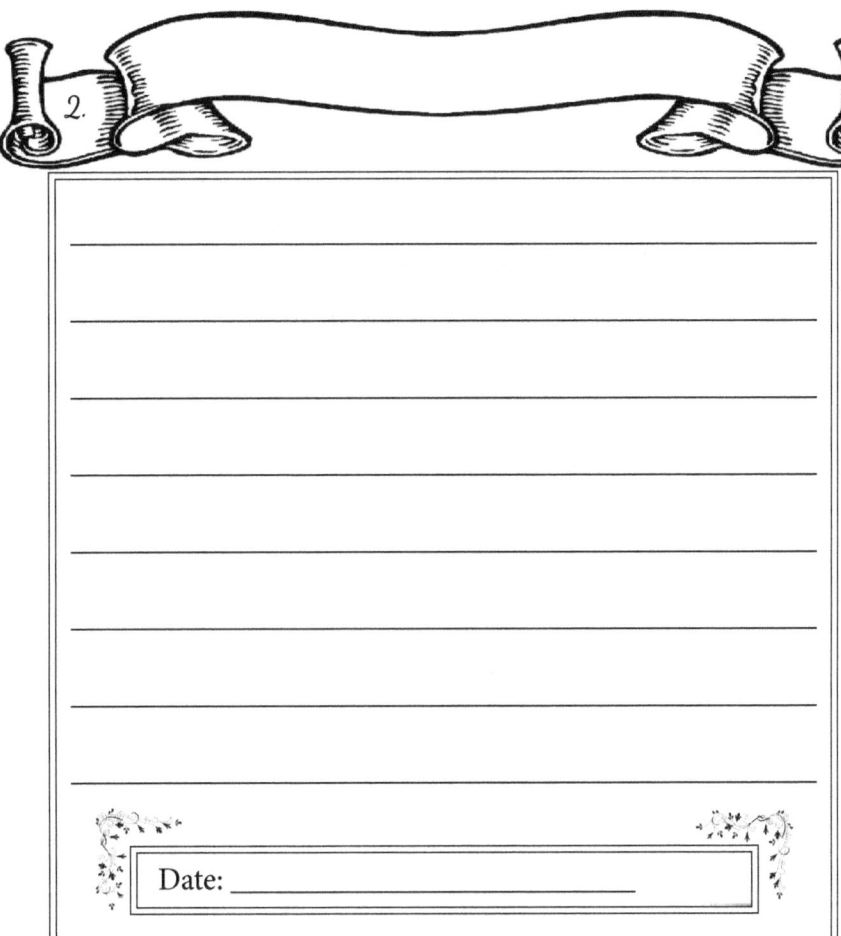

"I keep finding myself stifled by the company of others and then crippled by loneliness when I leave them. I am terrified and I don't even know of what, because I have lost everything already."

― Veronica Roth

What are you afraid of?

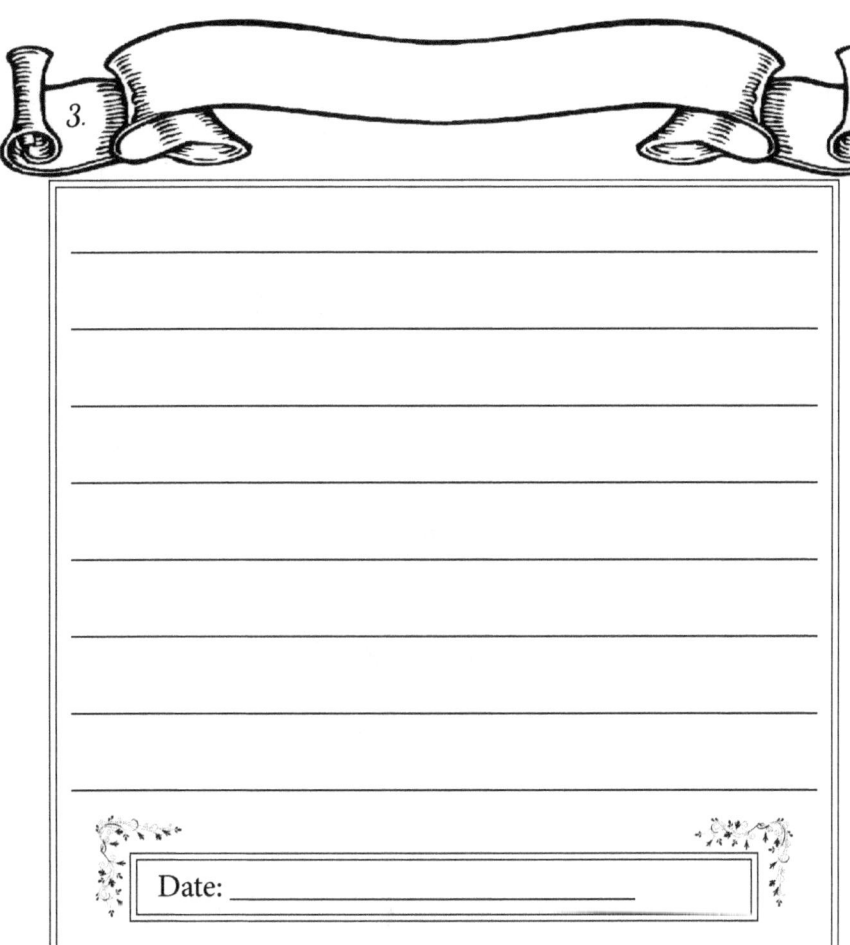

"Grief turns out to be a place none of us know until we reach it."

— *Joan Didion*

Describe your grief.

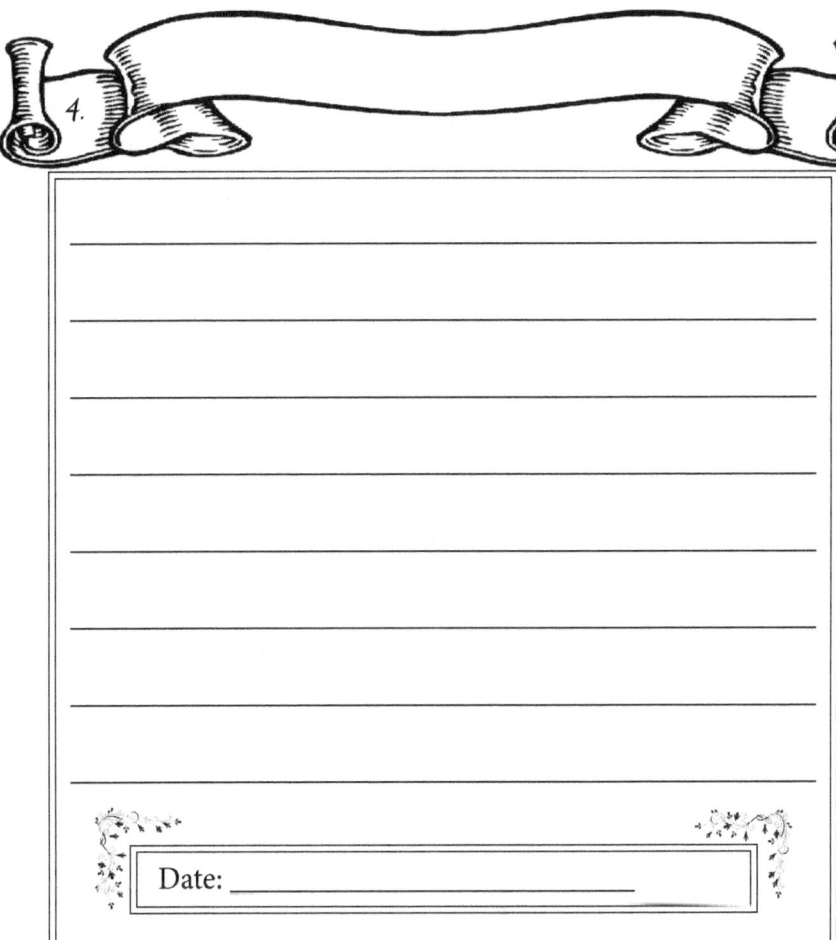

4.

Date: _____

"It is useless for me to describe to you how terrible Violet, Klaus, and even Sunny felt in the time that followed. If you have ever lost someone very important to you, then you already know how it feels, and if you haven't, you cannot possibly imagine it."

— *Lemony Snicket*

What do you want others to understand about *your* grief?

5.

Date: _____

"Never compare your insides to someone else's outsides."

— Rob Lowe

What resides in your heart and mind?

6.

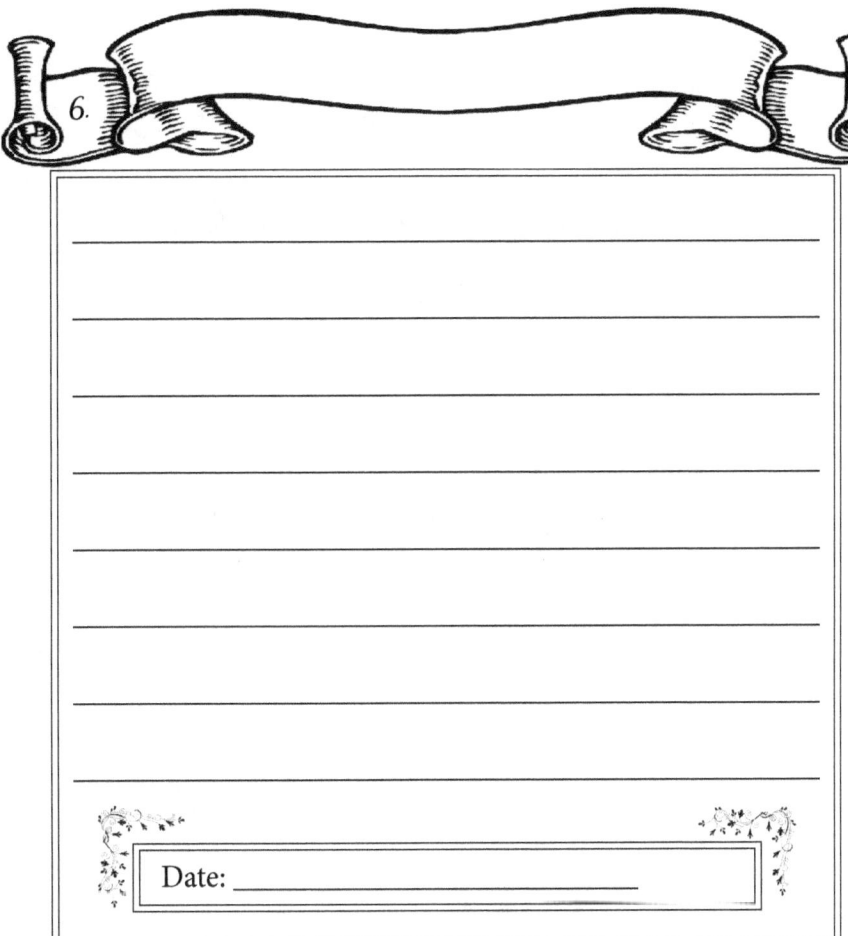

Date: _____

"Grief does not change you. It reveals you."

— *John Green*

How have you responded to your grief?

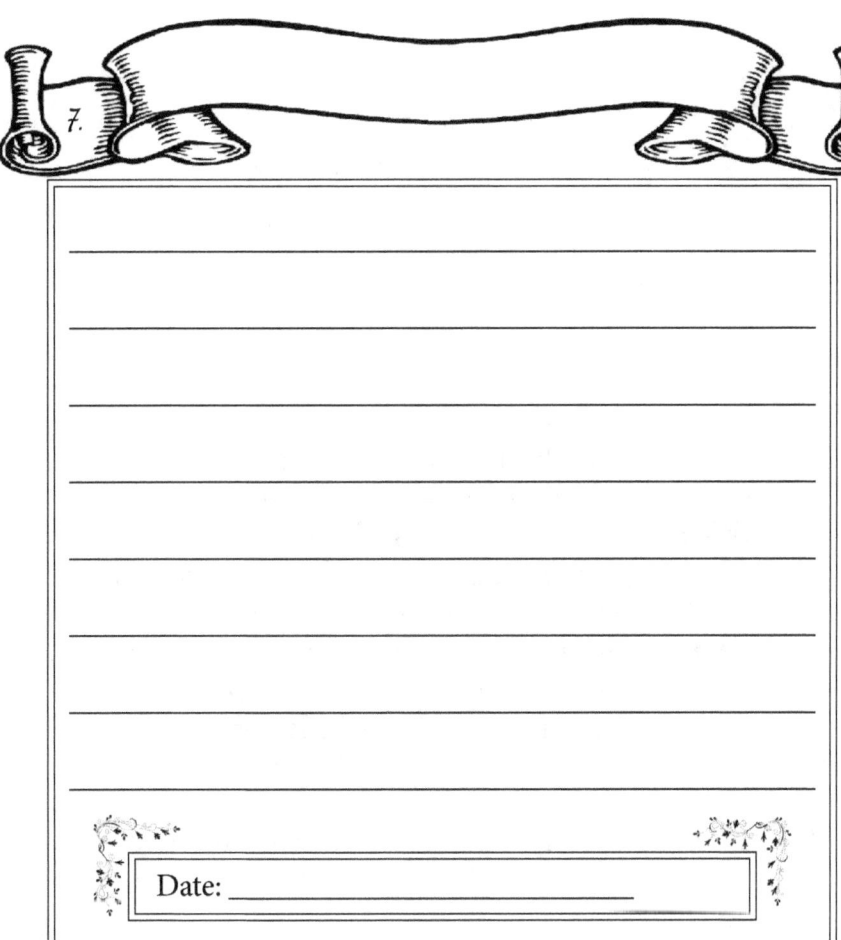

7.

Date: _____

*"I will not say: do not weep;
for not all tears are an evil."*

― J.R.R. Tolkien

Many quote Rumi in his encouragement of *'Don't grieve. Anything you lose comes round in another form'* or, similarly, Kilbran when he says, *'When you part from your friend, you grieve not, for that which you love most in him may be clearer in his absence, as the mountain to the climber is clearer from the plain.'*
Yet, such sentiment brings little comfort when in the grips of deep grief.

How often do you cry, and how do you feel afterwards?

"Only people who are capable of loving strongly can also suffer great sorrow, but this same necessity of loving serves to counteract their grief and heals them."

— Leo Tolstoy

"So it's true, when all is said and done, grief is the price we pay for love."

— E.A. Bucchianeri

What paradoxes are present in your life
that have become more pronounced with grief?

9.

Date: _____

"They say time heals all wounds, but that presumes the source of the grief is finite"

— Cassandra Clare

Deep grief can transition to less painful emotions
where abiding love is the reflection that remains.
Yet, this is on your timeline, no one else's.
Grief is a spectrum and a collage. It contains all our
emotions, sometimes at the same time.
When we lose someone dear,
the loss often will remain ever-present.
Moving on is impossible.
Moving forward is necessary.

What are your deepest wounds?
What, if anything, is helping them heal?

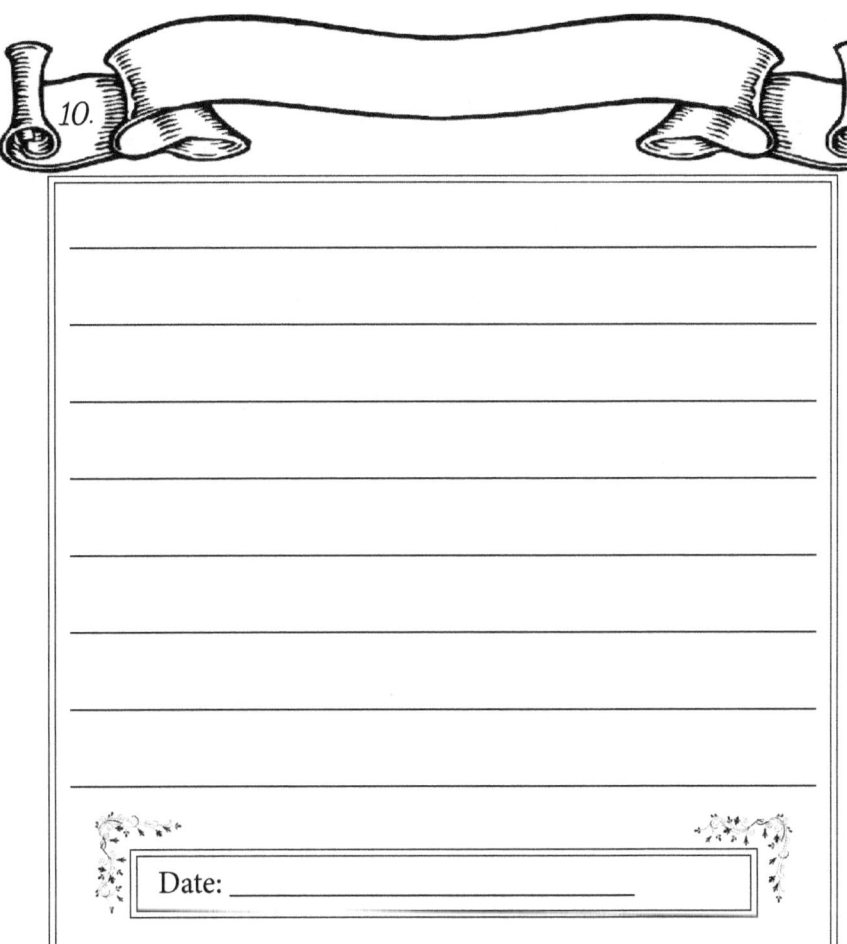

10.

Date: _____

"It's so curious: one can resist tears and 'behave' very well in the hardest hours of grief. But then someone makes you a friendly sign behind a window, or one notices that a flower that was in bud only yesterday has suddenly blossomed, or a letter slips from a drawer... and everything collapses."

— Colette

What innocent and innocuous things trigger your grief?

11.

Date:

"The worst type of crying wasn't the kind everyone could see--the wailing on street corners, the tearing at clothes. No, the worst kind happened when your soul wept and no matter what you did, there was no way to comfort it."

― Katie McGarry

What part of your grief feels inconsolable?

12.

Date: _____

"Now something so sad has hold of us that the breath leaves and we can't even cry."

— Charles Bukowski

What would you like to say to your breaking heart?
What would you say to someone else in your position?

13.

Date: _____

"In times of grief and sorrow I will hold you and rock you and take your grief and make it my own. When you cry I cry and when you hurt I hurt. And together we will try to hold back the floods to tears and despair and make it through the potholed street of life"

— Nicholas Sparks

You are not alone…but sometimes, we are alone….
Sometimes what we are experiencing is so foreign to the experiences of those closest to us that surrendering our grief into their hands feels more difficult than coping on our own. And, sometimes, we are, indeed, alone.
Life and living is complex.
Grief and grieving can seem insurmountable.

Who or what can you turn to with your grief?
What brings you hope and generates faith?

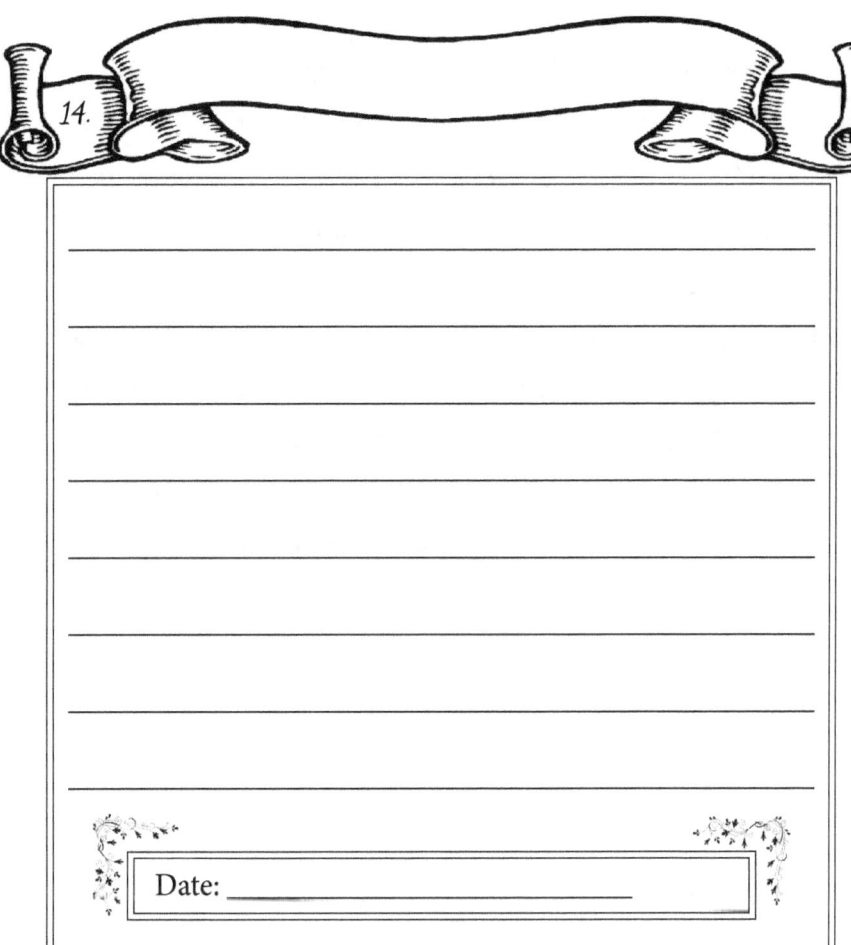

"No one ever told me that grief felt so like fear. I am not afraid, but the sensation is like being afraid. The same fluttering in the stomach, the same restlessness, the yawning. I keep on swallowing.

At other times it feels like being mildly drunk, or concussed. There is a sort of invisible blanket between the world and me. I find it hard to take in what anyone says. Or perhaps, hard to want to take it in. It is so uninteresting. Yet I want the others to be about me. I dread the moments when the house is empty. If only they would talk to one another and not to me."

— C.S. Lewis

What are your interactions with others like?

15.

Date: _____

"She was a genius of sadness, immersing herself in it, separating its numerous strands, appreciating its subtle nuances. She was a prism through which sadness could be divided into its infinite spectrum."

"It's so painful to think, and tell me, what did thinking ever do for me, to what great place did thinking ever bring me? I think and think and think, I've thought myself out of happiness one million times, but never once into it."

— Jonathan Safran Foer

What is the single most important thing to you right now?

16.

Date: _____

"*Grief can destroy you --or focus you.*

— Dean Koontz

Which path are you choosing?

17.

Date: _____

*"She heard him mutter,
'Can you take away this grief?'
'I'm sorry,' she replied. 'Everyone asks me.
And I would not do so even if I knew how.
It belongs to you. Only time and tears take away
grief; that is what they are for."*

― *Terry Pratchett*

You need to go into the Afterward when faced with a loss.
It is sometimes necessary to stay there for a time.
To go inward. To make peace with it, when possible.
Take comfort when it comes. And remember:
The Afterward is not meant to be permanent.
Accept that there is more than the Afterward.
There is the Next.
There is Life. There is Now.

What is the most sacred thing about *your* grief?

18.

Date: _____

"No matter how bad your heart is broken, the world doesn't stop for your grief."

— Faraaz Kazi

If you could have a retreat for the day,
what would it look like?

19.

Date: _____

*"Every man has his secret sorrows
which the world knows not."*

— *Henry Wadsworth Longfellow*

*"The whole world can become the enemy
when you lose what you love."*

— *Kristina McMorris*

What brings you joy, even amid your grief?

"Understanding is the first step to acceptance."

— J.K. Rowling

What is it that you must accept?

What will help you do so?

Date: _____

"When grief sits with you, its tropical heat
thickening the air, heavy as water
more fit for gills than lungs;
when grief weights you like your own flesh
only more of it, an obesity of grief,
you think, How can a body withstand this?
Then you hold life like a face
between your palms, a plain face,
no charming smile, no violet eyes,
and you say, yes, I will take you
I will love you, again."

— Ellen Bass

What everyday miracle recently surprised you?

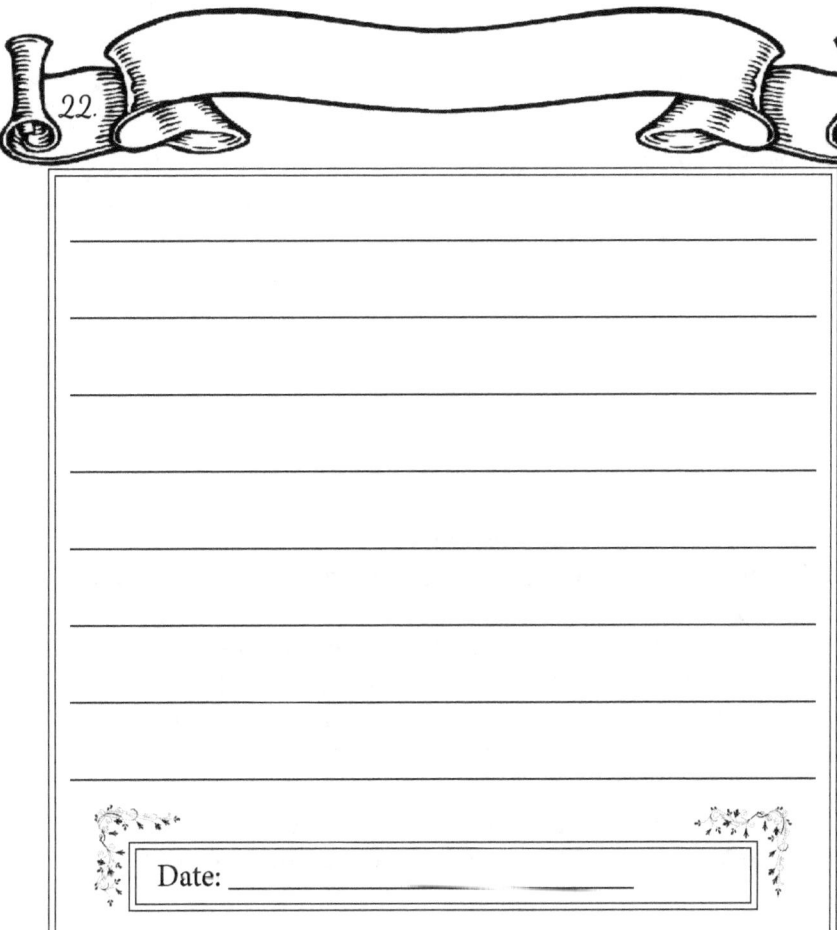

Date: _____

"There comes a day when you smile again, and you feel like a traitor. How dare I feel happy."

— Laurell K. Hamilton

We can experience joy alongside our grief, and do.
It can surprise us and even worry us when we have feelings of happiness. It can feel like a betrayal to who we are grieving. Be grateful for any joyful moments and feelings that occur during your times of grief. They will help you stay connected to your human experiences rather than be swept away by your grief.

Write about a recent happy moment.
Write about something or someone that makes you smile.

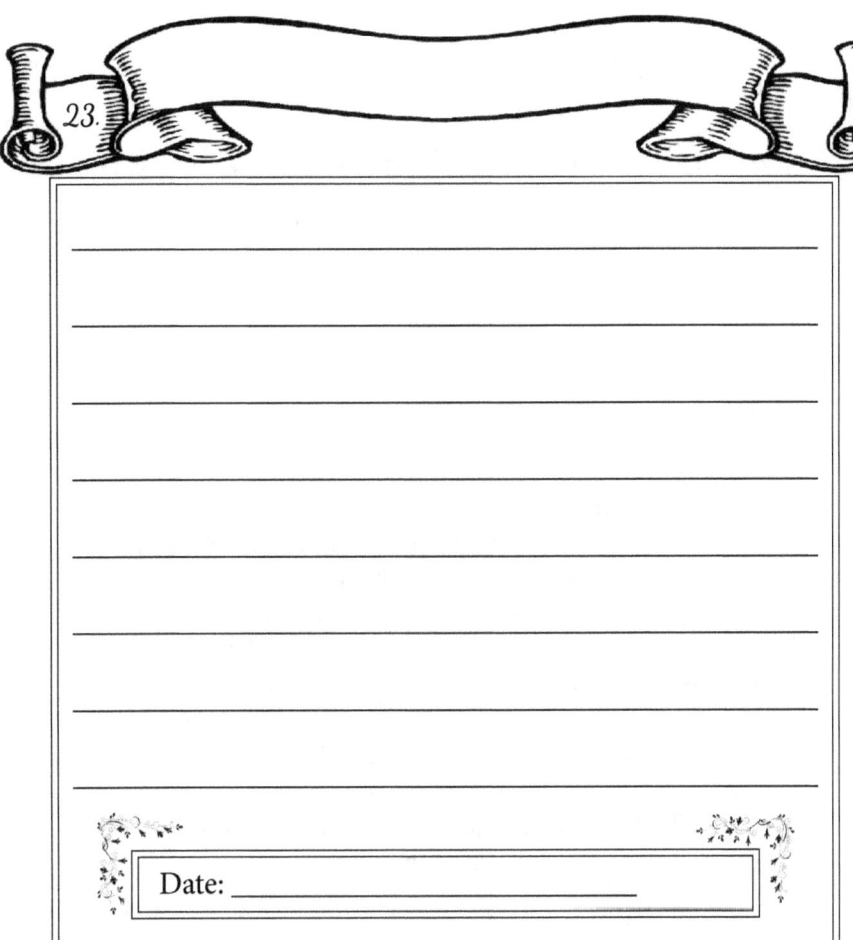

Date: _____

"You could grieve endlessly for the loss of time and the damage done therein."

— *Charles Frazier*

Time, a commodity impossible to trade for its actual value.
Time, a trust fund we cannot save for a rainy day.
Time, a gift that comes with freedom of will.
Time, gaining equity only in legacy.
Every moment, we get to choose where our Time reserve
goes, how we spend it, and who we allow to draw from it.

Your grief deserves your attention.
So does your life.
Where, to what and to whom do you wish
to dedicate your time?

"Let yourself be inert, wait till the incomprehensible power ... that has broken you restores you a little."

― Marcel Proust

You are not the same person you were before your grief. Returning to that person is impossible. How could it be anything but for your loss and your grief are part of you now. And, there is a fullness in that. Accepting and embracing this are an essential part of the transformation you are now going through.

What qualities do you notice sifting to the top of your personality that you are grateful for?
What shape is your belief structure taking?
What matters most to you?
Who are you becoming?

25.

Date: _____

*"And when I reveal my true heart,
not everyone is going to approve.
What I know now is that
I don't need them to."*

— Alicia Keys

Oftentimes with grief, there is a letting go.
A letting go of the willingness to be presided over
by other people's expectations and beliefs
about life, and about you.

What inherited ideas and ideals
are you letting go of now?
What truths are you embracing?

26.

Date: _____

"Come back. Even as a shadow, even as a dream."

— *Euripides*

The veil between grief and living is tangible.
It calls to you and beckons you forward
in your daytime and dreamtime.

What aspects about life are easiest, most comfortable,
perhaps even welcome, for you to come back to?

27.

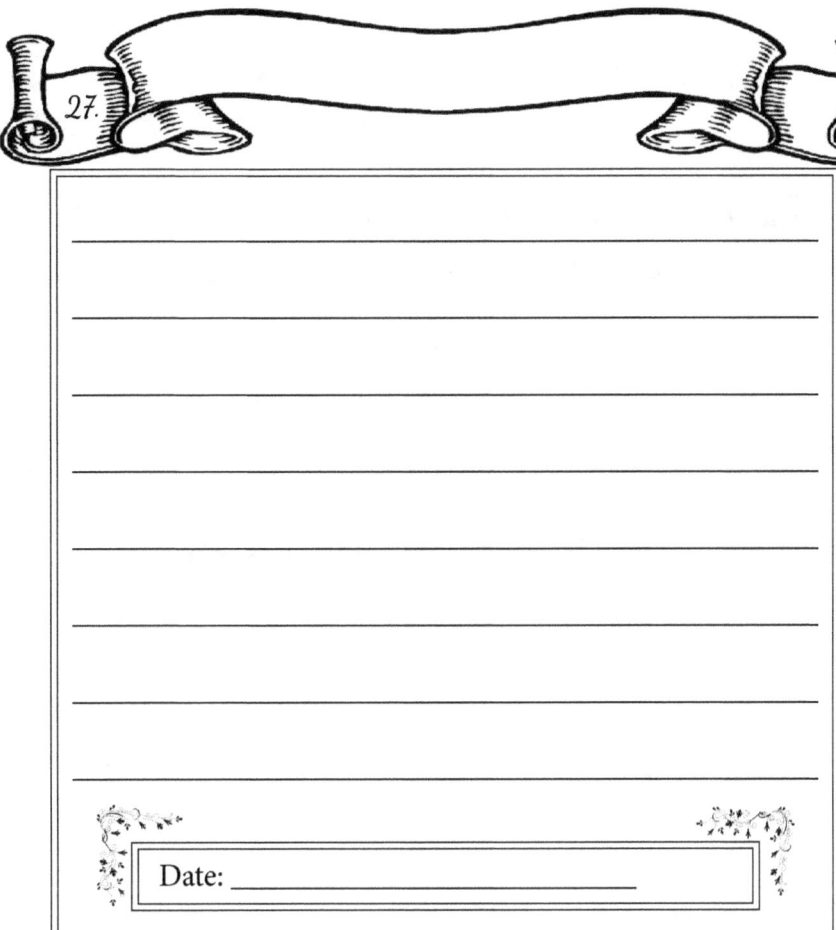

Date: _____

"The world always seems brighter when you've just made something that wasn't there before."

— Neil Gaiman

What creative things are you willing to say 'Yes' to?

28.

Date: _____

"The essential question is not, 'How busy are you?' but 'What are you busy at?' Are you doing what fulfills you?"

— Oprah Winfrey

What fulfills you?

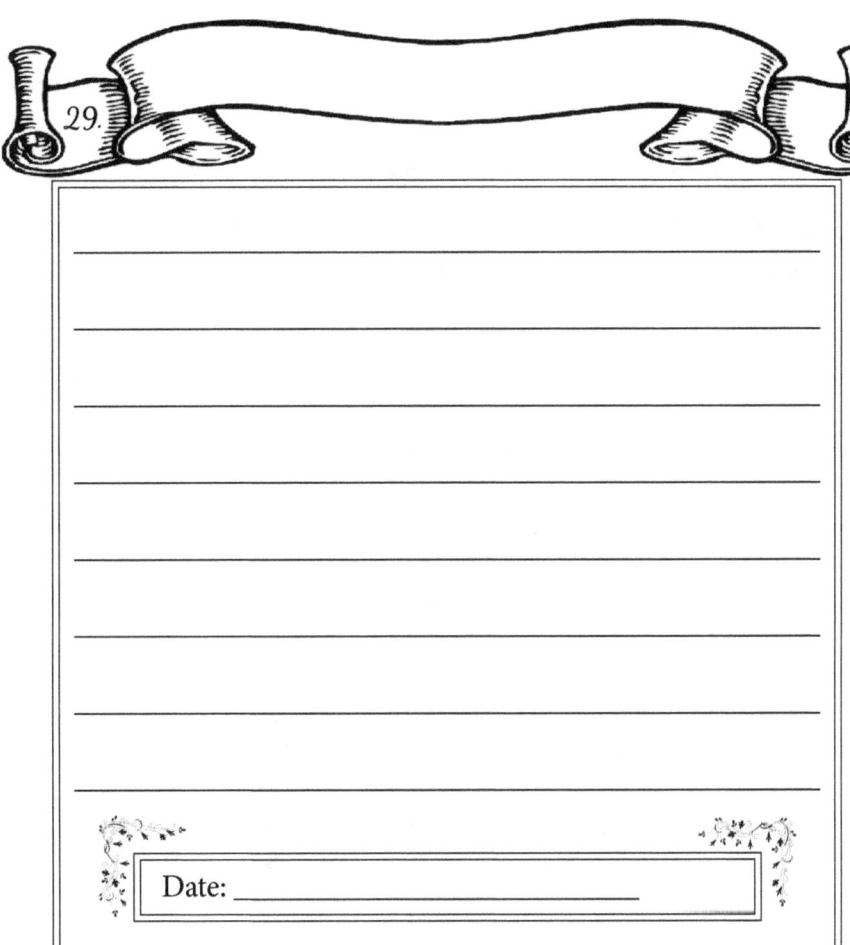

Date: _____

*"Whoever you are, no matter how lonely,
the world offers itself to your imagination,
calls to you like the wild geese, harsh and exciting –
over and over announcing your place
in the family of things."*

― Mary Oliver,

You deserve to live a full and happy life.
When in doubt, be in Nature.

Where is your favorite place to go to rejuvenate?
Describe how it makes you feel.

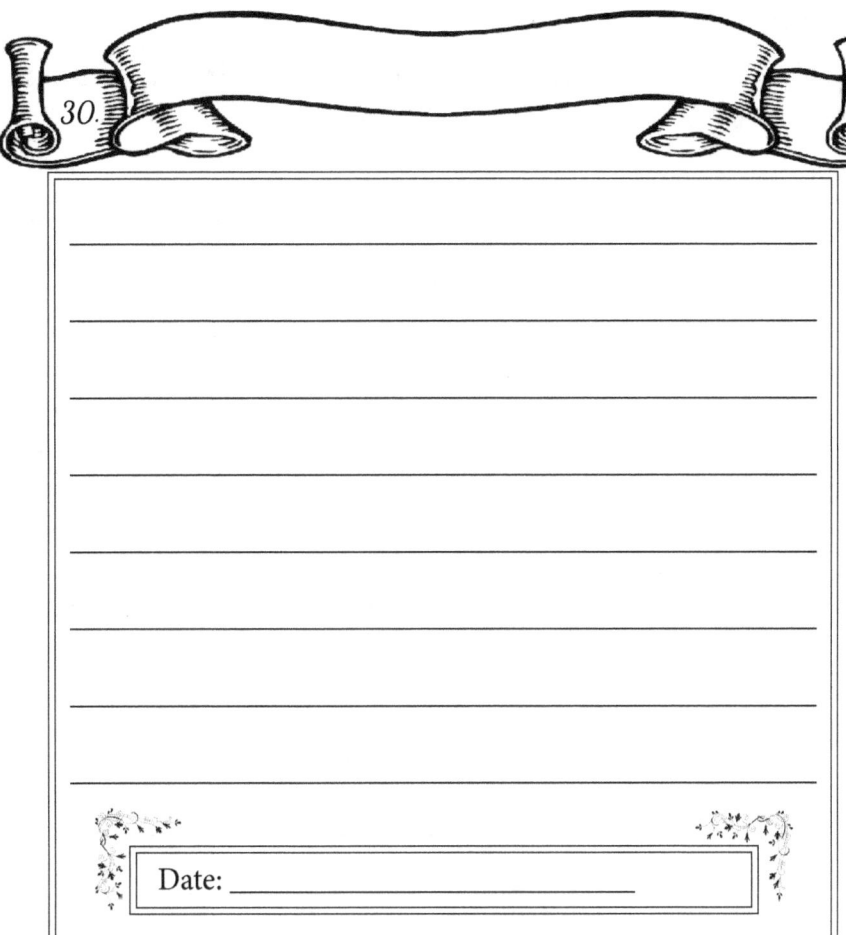

Reflections

What additional discernments have come through to you during these Blue Christmas prompts?

A Holiday Exercise

The next four pages contain several quotes from popular Christmas songs and movies. I invite you to close your eyes, take a breath, and point to a place on the page, then open your eyes and read the first quote you see. On a separate piece of paper, or in your journal, write about the thoughts, feelings and emotions you experience. Repeat this as often as you wish. Be sure to write your responses!

"It's the most wonderful time of the year!"

"It's beginning to look a lot like Christmas."

"I'm dreaming of a white Christmas, just like the ones I used to know."

"Christmas Eve will find me, where the love light gleams. I'll be home for Christmas, if only in my dreams."

"This is extremely important. Will you please tell Santa that instead of presents this year, I just want my family back." — Kevin McCallister (Macaulay Culkin) **"Home Alone"** (1990)

"I'll have a blue Christmas without you."

"We wish you a Merry Christmas and a Happy New Year!"

"Have yourself a merry little Christmas."

"Let it snow, let it snow, let it snow."

"There must have been some magic in that old silk hat they found, for when they placed it on his head, he began to dance around! Frosty the Snowman…"

"Rudolph the red-nosed reindeer, had a very shiny nose. And if you ever saw it, you would even say it glows."

"Maybe Christmas, he thought… doesn't come from a store. Maybe Christmas, perhaps… means a little bit more!" – Narrator (Boris Karloff) **"How The Grinch Stole Christmas"** (1966)

"Sleigh bells ring, are you listening? In the lane, snow is glistening. A beautiful sight, we're happy tonight. Walking in a winter wonderland."

"Jingle Bells, jingle bells, jingle all the way! Oh what fun it is to ride, in a one horse open sleigh."

"Deck the halls with boughs of holly, fa la la la la, la la la la."

"Simply having a wonderful Christmas time."

"It's Christmas Eve. It's the one night of the year when we all act a little nicer, we smile a little easier, we cheer a little more. For a couple of hours out of the whole year we are the people that we always hoped we would be." — Frank Cross (Bill Murray) **"Scrooged"** (1988)

"Joy to the world, the Lord is come, let Earth receive her King."

"Hark now, hear the angels sing, a King was born today."

"Away in a manger, no crib for a bed. The little Lord Jesus laid down his sweet head."

"'And this shall be a sign unto you; Ye shall find the babe wrapped in swaddling clothes, lying in a manger.' And suddenly there was with the angel a multitude of the heavenly host, praising God, and saying, 'Glory to God in the highest, and on earth peace, good will toward men.' That's what Christmas is all about, Charlie Brown." — Linus Van Pelt **"A Charlie Brown Christmas" (1965)**

"Silent night! Holy night! All is calm! All is bright!"

"O Christmas tree, O Christmas tree."

"How'd you like to spend Christmas, on Christmas Island?"

"Baby, it's cold outside…"

"Silver bells, silver bells, it's Christmas time in the city. Ring-a-ling, hear them ring, soon it will be Christmas Day."

"Do you hear what I hear?"

"Rain drops on rose and whiskers on kittens. Bright copper kettles and warm woolen mittens. Brown paper packages tied up with strings. These are a few of my favorite things."
– Maria von Trapp *(Julie Andrews)* **"The Sound of Music"** *(1965)*

"On the first day of Christmas, my true love gave to me: a partridge in a pear tree."

"Jingle bell, Jingle bell, Jingle bell rock."

"Rocking around the Christmas tree, have a happy holiday."

"Every time a bell rings an angel gets his wings."
"Look, Daddy. Teacher says, every time a bell rings an angel gets his wings." — Zuzu Bailey (Karolyn Grimes) **"It's a Wonderful Life"** *(1946)*

"And so, I'm offering this simple phrase to kids from one to 92. Although it's been said many times, many ways, Merry Christmas to you."

"I saw Mommy kissing Santa Claus."

"So kiss me on this cold December night."

"All I want for Christmas is You."

Thoughts for Contemplation
Including musings, poetry, meditations, teachings and prayers.

Listen
Breathe in each morning the magick of Life;
Breathe out each evening deep gratitude for living.
And Listen to the Call of the Universe
in every interaction
in every curve in the road
in every commitment to task
in every covenant of relationship
in every whispered word
in every meditation
in every prayer
in every song
Listen.

May we enter the Holy Quiet:
That place of Being that is within us,
and through us, and beyond us.

Consider with me this:

There is a divine echo that whispers
within every heart.
Indeed, that every soul carries with it
the echo of a intrinsic intimacy.
An original echo that is brought fourth
through time from original source.
A primal source where we are all One.
And we carry the essence of this original echo
as a talisman of our divinity.

There exists a place in our hearts where intimacy has
no limit and love has no barrier.

When one listens to the Universe,
the Universe listens back.

Do you Pray?
I pray daily and throughout the day.
My life is a life of prayer.
My journey with prayer has been
an ever evolving one.
At present prayer to me is surrender and gratitude.
The first, surrender, is in communion with,
and experience of, the Holy.
The second, deep gratitude for the Holy and the
many gifts in my life. The outward appearance of
such prayers can be formal or spontaneous:
intentional moments of stillness and silence, visualization, or active with writing, creating art, chanting
or singing or drawing down the moon, walking in
the woods and along the river, speaking out loud my
heart's desires or giving a blessing, it is the lullabies
with my child each night….Prayer is even found in
doing the dishes at my kitchen sink,
and dancing in my living room.

May you live Life like a Prayer.

I believe that prayer can be as diverse as that which we call Holy and can be made manifest through words, thoughts and deeds, such as daily acts of grace and gratitude.

I turn to prayer in gratitude and also in surrender when circumstances are beyond my control. Sometimes my prayers manifest in writings and visualizations; oftentimes the simple act of touching my hand to my heart and humming (kind of like the Om) places me in conscious union with the divine.

My guess is, that we each have something that we feel is Holy. And I urge you to turn to that first. When feeling vulnerable, when feeling scared, when feeling like you are just not quite feeling like yourself,
Turn to that which you identify as Holy, identify as Sacred.

When we live life as a prayer,
our reactions to situations and to people
become subtle,
even unconscious,
manifestations of the prayer
we bring in to the world.

We begin to recognize the beauty blossoming
in our own hearts and minds.
And as that beauty blossoms,
we recognize with clarity
the callings of our heart;
the *callings* from God.
And it is this,
hearing and answering our callings,
which transforms our otherwise transient lives
into union with the Divine.
This union becomes evident in the transfiguration
of our thoughts,
and our emotions.
And when this happens
we no longer need to clench when faced with
challenging situations
or difficult people.

Because we belong together,
we are called to exercise compassion
towards each other,
and, towards ourselves.

It is the act of compassion that awakens us
to bring forth our best gifts to our community.

It is the act of self-compassion that emboldens us
to be brave,
and by 'be brave'
I mean it is self-compassion that allows us
to be vulnerable enough
to give over our burdens and our sorrows
into the tender loving care of our community.

Shared vulnerability,
sharing our most joyful experiences,
along with our sorrows,
this is what builds strength.

Strength in our community.
Strength in each of us.

May we build such Beloved Communities.

Life is center-oriented.

A supportive force, designed
to bring us naturally into alignment.
The catch?
It requires our active participation.
In return, it gives us the needed gravitational pull to
center.
It does not require us to reject any part of our selves.
Yet is does demand we have a clear center to orient
us.
With that in balance, we can be confident that
we can align all parts as we hold close to our center
with seemingly effortless grace.

The sustainability of the peace, joy, and purpose
we discover in our hearts
is strengthened (and weakened)
by the people and communities we choose
to surround ourselves with.

In myriad ways, we connect and affect.

Whatever is inside of us continually flows outward;
Whatever is outside us continually flows inward.

If life on the outside is presenting
things to be grateful for,
gather the gratitude for those
into your Heart's storehouse.

If life on the outside is presenting things
that cause you to feel fear or sadness,
reach into your heart and find
the place where your love
and your gratitude
and your peace
and peace of mind
resides
and bring that forward.

Because the world needs it.
You need it.

To have resolve is to be gifted
unyielding firmness or endurance.

To practice resolve is to act
with robust commitment that is
made possible by a strong,
healthy, dynamic faith.

May it be known
That I retrieve all I am
To do all I am meant to.
From this moment on.
So mote it be.

May your life be filled with a kaleidoscope of color
and beauty and joy.

May we be like the trees
and transform our world
with every breath.

May deep listening begin to take place from every
corner of each controversial discussion.
Deep listening without accusations.
Deep listening with the goal
of understanding each other.
May we remember we are a people of Love.

May we understand that
we are capable of being loved,
no matter what wounds we still carry,
no matter what mistakes we still make.
May we know that
we are capable of loving generously,
even beyond our wildest imaginations.
May we see
beyond the shadow and into the Soul.
Amen and Blessed Be.

As a society, we treat Time as if we have
a surplus attached to a lavish line of credit
and syphon it into a plethoric gluttony
of distractions.
We are either numb to,
or feel the pressing weight of,
the tedious excess expected of our Time.
Time, a commodity
impossible to trade for its actual value.
Time, a trust fund
we cannot save for a rainy day.
Time, a gift
that comes with freedom of will.
Time, gaining equity
only in legacy.

How important it is to make every moment count.

The Dark Season

We are at the threshold of the Seasons,
the doorway to the Year,
when the Veil is thin,
and time passes amorphously.
We turn inward as the Darkness beckons us.
We welcome the warmth of the fire,
contemplating the mysteries of the Unseen.
We honor the soft ache in our hearts
for those we have lost:
the people,
the dreams.
And we rest.
For rest we must, to heal.
This is the cycle of death and rebirth;
release and renewal.
We cherish this time
as the lessons it offers
penetrate our knowing.
May we breathe in wisdom
and breathe out patience.

Instead of one call to action after another,
how about a call to rest,
to be still,
to go within,
to look each other in the eyes,
to hold each other,
to be with one another.

What I am suggesting,
What I'm imploring,
And what I am asking...
...is for you to give yourself permission to rest.

Relax.
Unclench.
Breathe.

Sacred.
Benevolent.
Loving.

Moving forward is necessary;
"moving on" is impossible.

Our loved-one's death was more than a moment;
their life is more than a memory.

Their existence is ever-present
as they shape our lives even now.

The Afterward is a place we all must travel to
on our paths towards wholeness and healing.
The Afterward in not meant to be permanent
Accept that there is more than the Afterward.
There is the Next.
There is Life.
There is Now.

Sabbatical Thinking

If in the fabric of our human lives
we built our organizations,
our communities,
our nations,
with the sentiment that we are indeed One,
we would begin to weave together lifestyles,
and cultures,
and ways of being that support,
and lift up,
nurture and nourish such Oneness.
In such a society,
we would install extended times of rest
and enrichment and sabbatical and retreat.
For everyone.

Love the Land You're With.

Doing so creates an embodied relationship with Nature.

If you live near the ocean, you can connect with the resonance of Her rhythms, finding both strength and healing there. Immerse in her wisdom. Enjoy the Oceans' sandy beaches and weathered cliffs. They provide long moments of reflection and inspiration. The metaphysical aspects of our souls open in Her presence. Unimaginable horizons open to us as the inescapable reality of the vastness of Life is before us each day and every night.

Inland you can find lakes and mountains that ground us in this place in Time, while providing us insights on the legacies of those who came before us, and the ones that will follow. In their stillness and aliveness, the mountains, the lake, the land and trees and fields that surround us guide us to embrace a deeper connection with Earth and with Spirit. If you live inward, both literally and symbolically, you can experience an ever-evolving transformation and awakening. Inland Life provides us with the opportunity to grow and to harvest as we work with the soil of the Land. Many find that inland they are nurtured and more nurturing.

Restoring Harmony

When what we recognize as disharmony materializes, especially when the disharmony creates physical isolation from the people we love, the places we like to spend time, and the routines and rituals we've organized our lives around, we can feel deeply disconnected.
Disconnected from that which we hold dear.
Disconnected from our own self assuredness and self awareness.
Disconnected from where we draw our faith.
This disconnected feeling feels like chaos to us.
Disrupting the harmony we recognize as holy.
As sacred. As safe.
Yet if we can still the emotional storm that is rising.
If we can locate calmness in our bodies, in our beings, we can restore the harmony.
As we cultivate this practice of weaving harmony from within the chaos, we become the conductor in the symphony of our emotions. This does not mean the chaos disappears entirely. Nor that we receive answers we like to all the things we have questions about. But it makes space, intentionally so, for us to navigate effectively within what Life has presented us with.

The Triage of Grief

They sat with me for hours in this spot.
Sometimes talking. Much of the time just being still,
gazing at Nature's tranquil beauty and
listening to the sounds of the Lake.

For some this may look like healing.
I know with experienced certainty it is not.
Not yet.
This, this is the perpetual triage of raw grief.

Keep the body still.
Regulate the breath.
Quiet the mind.
Assess the wound.
Allow tears, laughter or lethargy to come.
Keep in check the anger.
When there is energy, do something useful,
purposeful.
Ardently cradle the sorrow when it assails.
Repeat.

About the Publisher

Matrika Press is an independent publishing house dedicated to publishing works in alignment with transformational religious and spiritual values and principles.

Matrika Press publishes anthologies, memoirs, poetry, prayer and ritual manuscripts, and other books (both fiction and nonfiction) to bring meaning and transformation to the world. A primary goal of Matrika Press is to publish stories and works that would otherwise remain untold. We also resurrect out-of-print manuscripts to ensure our historical works remain accessible.

Why the name "Matrika"?
It is said that Matrika is the intrinsic energy or sound vibration of the 50 letters of the Sanskrit alphabet called "the mothers of creation." The Goddess Kali Ma used the letters to form words, and from the words formed all things. This aligns with scriptures that assert "in the beginning was the Word," and in other sacred texts that affirm people of all backgrounds and faiths agree: Words are powerful. More than that: Their vibrations are creative forces; they bring all things into being.

Matrika Press titles are automatically made available to tens of thousands of retailers, libraries, schools, and other distribution and fulfillment partners, including Amazon, Barnes & Noble, Chapters/Indigo (Canada), and other well-known book retailers and wholesalers across North America, and in the United Kingdom, Europe, Australia and New Zealand and other Global partners.

For more information, visit:

www.MatrikaPress.com
www.RSOTDE.org/MatrikaPress

About the Author

Rev. Dr. "Twinkle" Marie Manning is an interfaith minister, skilled ritualist, liturgist and artist who has been leading workshops and seminars in the secular and spiritual worlds for more than two decades. She actively develops and leads programs that nourish spirituality. Her rituals, reflections and poetry have been included internationally in all manner of worship services and publications.

The series of *Blessing Books* is among the most popular of her publishing endeavors. Other published works include the *Women of Spirit* anthology series, *Intentional Visualization*, *Be Like the Trees*, *Restore Us to Memory*, the *Pulpit of Peace* collection, and *Living Life as a Prayer*.

Her community ministry, affectionately known as *Twinkle's Place,* has grown to encompass multifaceted offerings, including wedding and funeral officiating and the emergence of retreat centers, sanctuaries and intentional communities.

www.TwinklesPlacc.org
www.MatrikaPress.com/twinkle-marie-manning
www.RSOTDE.org/titles-by-twinkle-marie-manning
www.EmpoweringWomenTV.org/founder

Other Works by this Author

Women of Spirit, Exploring Sacred Paths of Wisdom Keepers is a compilation of women sojourners, sages, mystics, witches, shaman, medicine women, ministers, philosophers, therapists, life coaches, yogis, and more.
Their journeys.
Their stories.
Their teachings and practices.
Essays, Poetry, Art, Rituals and Prayers. This anthology is full of useful tools and powerful messages for everyone who is on a spiritual journey to embrace and enjoy. Beloved Contributors include:

- Anna Huckabee Tull
- Bernadette Rombough
- Deb Elbaum • Deborah Diamond
- Debra Wilson Guttas • Grace Ventura
- Janeen Barnett • JoAnne Bassett
- Judy Ann Foster • Julie Matheson
- Kate Early • Kate Kavanagh
- Katherine Glass • Kris Oster
- Lea M. Hill • Meghan Gilroy
- Morwen Two Feathers • Rustie MacDonald
- Shamanaca • Sharon Hinckley
- Shawna Allard • Shiloh Sophia
- Susan Feathers • Tiffany Cano
- Tory Londergan
- "Twinkle" Marie Manning
- Tziporah Kingsbury • Valerie Sorrentino

www.MatrikaPress.com/women-of-spirit

Divinely inspired. Practically written. *Living Life as a Prayer* presents a transformational theology that is accessible to everyone who wishes to embrace life in gratitude and grace. As a spiritual guidebook, *Living Life as a Prayer* outlines principles and practices to help us more deeply connect with that which we personally and uniquely identify as holy.

In her seminal work, Rev. Manning shepherds readers toward realizing our intrinsic connection to each other, and to the Divine.

BLESSING BOOK SERIES

Uniquely designed to be journals, spiritual exploration tools and self-led retreats, *Blessing Books* can be used to mark a milestone such as a significant birthday or important season of your life. *Blessing Books* can help you process a loss or transition. It can be where you express your gratitude or your grief, and where you affirm what's present and next in your life. Wherever you are on your journey, and in both times of joy and in times of sorrow, may these books serve you well.

Pulpit of Peace is part of the *a Pocketful Book Series*.

This book features excerpts from Rev. Dr. "Twinkle" Marie Manning's sermons, as well as glimpses of her poetry, meditations, rituals and reflections. Common themes of her ministry and writings found in this book include: Building The Beloved Community; Möbius Life; Sacred Economy; Living Life as a Prayer.

www.MatrikaPress.com/ twinkle-marie-manning

Other Books by Matrika Press

www.MatrikaPress.com

Featured Titles

The Circle Model of Shared Leadership by Elizabeth Fisher is a concrete group facilitation process that balances achieving tasks with emotional bonding. By using this book you will:
- Learn ways to bring a collection of individuals together, in a committee, board, or activist project, uniting each one's efforts which are equally valued.
- Develop skills critical to honing participatory decision-making and supporting the soul of the group, which must be kept strong if the group is to accomplish its goals.
- Discover important principles, practices and tools that support effective collaboration within and among all the levels of organizations.

www.MatrikaPress.com/the-circle-model

Sue Roy Humphries' historic aggregation work featuring behind-the-scenes documentation of sci-fi and horror classics in theatrical make-up effects has been all but hidden from the world for decades. Originally published in 1980, **Making a Monster** has been long out of print.

Matrika Press is delighted to revive this manuscript on its 40th Anniversary in response to those seeking a comprehensive montage of this highly creative aspect of filmmaking.

Making a Monster reveals the artistic secrets of your favorite vintage fantasy films. This book is filled with detailed accounts of the early era of makeup processes and ingenious solutions to the challenges of pre-CGI Visual FX.

While the manuscript reveals the trade and techniques of transforming some of Hollywood's most beautiful and beloved icons into infamous villains and fantastical creatures, its content also lends a lens unto the human psyche, including that of choosing what to believe in. Said another way, choosing One's Faith.

www.MatrikaPress.com/making-a-monster

Twinkle's Children's Book Series!

The Mora Mulberry Series is about a little girl who lives by the ocean on a farm in Maine with her mother.
Mora and her friends are so happy to share their adventures and lessons with you!
Cardinal Magic is the first book in the series. It is about kindness and welcoming new friends. It also offers strategies to help overcome stress.

www.TwinklesPlace.org/MoraMulberry

Empowering WOMEN
Salon Gatherings
&
Signature Events

"Twinkle" Marie Manning
is the founder of the
Empowering Women TV project.
She and her friends host these amazing gatherings! If you would like to attend,
or Host one,
in your community, visit:

www.EmpoweringWomenTV.org

Join Twinkle in-person or online!

☐ If you are seeking spiritual solace, Twinkle posts regularly on her website and social media pages.

☐ If you are a congregation or group wishing to download her sermons, meditations, readings and poems - Or wish to have her as a guest, please reach out to her directly.

☐ If you are a retreat leader seeking to collaborate, please contact Twinkle with your proposal.

www.TwinklesPlace.org

Holding your grief sacred during the holiday season.
www.TwinklesPlace.org/blue-christmas

ISBN: 978-1-946088-27-7

www.ingramcontent.com/pod-product-compliance
Lightning Source LLC
Chambersburg PA
CBHW081753100526
44592CB00015B/2408